Self-Publish Without Spending Money
By Matthew Davenport

Note from the author:

We greatly appreciate you taking the time to read our work. Please consider leaving a review wherever you bought the book, or telling your friends about Self-Publish Without Spending Money, to help us spread the word. Thank you so much for your support.

Part 1: Introduction

What This Book Is

"$1,800.00 for the first book," the elderly woman who had trapped me at my counter was saying.

Until that point, I had managed to pretend to listen very well. I was an e-reader salesman and tethered to my e-reader display counter. In theory it was a great sales tactic, but in reality every geriatric book-lover saw me as the perfect target for chatting up. I was literally a captive audience.

For that reason, I had become quite adept at feigning interest while my mind wandered, but when this woman with her ridiculously fake, jet-black hair mentioned that she had spent $1,800.00 to self-publish her novel, my attention surged to the surface.

"You paid $1,800.00 to self-publish your first novel?" I asked without hiding any of my incredulity.

She looked at me as if I had just told her how ridiculous her hair actually looked. "Well, what did you have to pay?"

It was no surprise that she knew I had recently self-published a novel. My coworkers had found that when chatty folks who had published a book came into the store it was easier to send them to Mr. Caged-and-Afraid. When customers walked up to me carrying on about their novels it usually started with something similar to, "You published a book? That's great! Let me tell you about mine."

Cher's Grandmother was no exception.

"Well," I answered. "I didn't spend anything."

She scoffed at me before asking, "What did *that* get you?"

I was still new to the game then, so I was preparing to be embarrassed by how far behind the curve I really was. I mean, if someone just spent almost two grand on their book, they must know something that I don't.

...right?

"Well, my book is on Amazon's Kindle store and the Barnes and Noble Nook. Plus, you can order it online from about 10 different retailers, including Amazon and B&N."

Her eyes went wide and she demanded, "How did you get it onto the Nook and into Barnes and Noble?"

It was my turn to hesitate with shock.

What did she mean, "How?" She went through a professional self-publishing company. She paid more money than I had seen in my bank account at any one time, and she was just bragging about her process. How was she confused?

"I...put them there..." Was all that I could muster before she began saying that it must be because I work at a book store and have "connections."

Finding myself, I explained, "Amazon and Barnes and Noble both have really easy platforms for uploading your book to their e-readers. It took me about half an hour. I also went through a group," I grabbed a pen for her at this point and jotted down, "called Lulu, and they helped me make the physical book and put it up on Amazon." I snapped my fingers at that point, as I remembered that I hadn't paid nothing to get my book published. "Lulu does cost $25 at that point if you want to get it into other book stores besides Amazon."

When I added, "That was it," her face grew an intense shaded of red. I couldn't tell if it was anger, embarrassment, or a mixture of both.

I asked her what her cash had gotten her. She explained that she got a bunch of postcards with her book and description on it, 10 copies of her book to hand-sell, and her book put onto only Amazon. She didn't get an e-book.

I found out the name of that group that she went through (a very popular group I later learned), but to avoid saying anything negative about anyone capable of getting lawyers involved, I'll avoid naming it here.

Needless to say, that was the first time I realized that by just using my own elbow grease and do-it-yourself nature, I didn't have to spend any money to get my book published.

I started out my writing career already $1,800.00 in the black.

Not bad, Mr. Davenport.

Of course, I was still eating microwave burritos for dinner, but heck, it was still a good start.

That's what this book is about. There are a lot of ways to go about getting your book in front of your readers, I just happened to be a cheap bastard who didn't want to spend any money on the process. In doing so, I found *my* way for getting my book in front of my readers.

While money, as in everything, can grease the process and make it easier in some places, you don't need it to make your dreams come true.

This book is about achieving your goals without spending any money.

What This Book Isn't

I've sat in on several classes on how other people have gone about publishing (both traditionally and self-publishing) their novels, and every time the conversation devolves into the same handful of topics.

- How do you come up with strong and believable characters?
- Do you backup your work on the cloud?
- Do you plot your stories first, or just sit down and start writing?
- Are Pen Names important?
- Should my novel be in the first-person or third-person narrative?
- What tools must you have with you?
- Do you listen to music when you write?
- Should I stop and edit my story as I go, or wait until I'm done?
- etc...etc...etc...

They just keep going and I contemplate giving the teacher an Oscar for Best Performance as they continue to show interest in these questions.

The reason?

The class is about publishing your work, not writing it, and all of those questions are inevitably about writing.

This book isn't about writing your book. If you're reading these pages, your book should already be written and saved wherever the heck you chose to save it.

In order to avoid these questions before they can occur, here's how I write a book:

- I jot the idea down into Evernote.

- It sits until I have time to start that idea.

- When I'm ready, I plot it out, with a pen in an Evernote Moleskine notebook.

- After each chapter is plotted, I scan the pages of my notebook into my Evernote.

- After each chapter is plotted, I'll write the first draft of the chapter in Evernote. (Sensing a theme? I like Evernote).

- When a chapter is done, I email it to a friend of mine who does my edits.

- When the story is done, I go back and read over her edits. She and I will go over the book a few times.

- Done.

That's my process. For more details you can check out my blog http://davenportwrites.com where I have detailed my process about four different times.

Also, feel free to check out Evernote. They don't pay me, but they probably should. I spout the awesomeness of Evernote everywhere I go. It is an invaluable tool.

Now that we have that out of our systems, let's review:

- This book is about getting your works published and marketed for free.

- This book is not about the writing process.

Are we clear?
Good.

Part 2: Advantages Of Self-Publishing

Why Would I?

Years ago, in the distant age of pre-early 2000's, self-publishing was a dirty word. A stigma of "not-good-enough" was as attached to the word as firmly as thick glasses with tape on the bridge were attached to the word "nerd."

The great news is that both words (*self-published* and *nerd*) have stepped into their own over the last few years. Not only can nerds such as myself be considered cool, but we can also publish novels and make more money than our traditionally published counterparts.

That's another set of words that I should define: Traditionally published. I'll be using it a good amount in this book and you should probably be aware of what I mean.

Being Traditionally Published means that you sent out the query letters and they happened to catch the attention of an agent. That agent, in turn, managed to use your manuscript to get the attention of a publisher who wanted to put your book on bookshelves. There's a lot of hard work in getting traditionally published, and anyone who accomplishes that has my unwavering respect.

By saying that, I'm not saying that Self-Publishing your work isn't a lot of hard work. Choosing to self-publish isn't taking the easy road, it's only taking a different road.

The benefits of getting traditionally published are numerous. The satisfaction is the first thing that pops into my head. When you find out that someone has just read your manuscript and wants to add their name to it in whatever way they can, that gives you a sense of otherworldly accomplishment. It is as if someone, up near where the gates are made of pearl, looked down at you and said, "You're alright, kid..."

The other benefits are more worldly than that, of course. You get a bunch of cash up front, which is very cool. You also get someone (your agent) who is constantly encouraging you to write more. Some people don't see a nag as a benefit, but I do. The agent can also introduce you to editors and publishers, who all want to help you get your book completed. They become your production team, and will help you to get what you want.

Unfortunately, the positives of getting a traditional book deal are greatly out-classed by the positives of self-publishing.

The big difference is that you get paid a lot less in getting traditionally published. A quick Google search asking for the differences between traditional and self-publishing put this right at the top. When you get traditionally published, you have a whole team of professionals and they all cost money. Unfortunately, you are the one who pays that money. From each sale of each book, you'll only get the industry average of 15% of the total book cost.

That sucks.

Comparatively, self-publishing has very few other people involved. Publishing platforms that you would use usually give you a return of anywhere from 70%-85% back on each sale.

That's awesome.

A lot of people think that that 15% from traditional publishing is worth it because the publisher and agent will help with a lot of the marketing as well. That's not the case.

I know an author who went the traditional route and at first he thought that was great, until he realized that he still had to do all of the work. His publisher gave him a few postcards and a flyer with his book on it, but he still had to order copies and do all of his own marketing. He wasn't very internet savvy, so he had to learn the social media sites, and the most that his traditional publisher does for him is to retweet his links when he posts them.

The next big difference is rights ownership. When you sign on with a publisher and agent, your contract is going to include a transfer of the rights of your story. This makes sense from a business perspective and protects the publisher from any other deals you might be trying to make with characters they've paid you for, such as movie or comic book deals.

This doesn't work to your advantage, though. If your publisher has a spat with a major distributor (i.e.: Go ahead and Google: Amazon and Hachette), then your books get pulled from those shelves and you can't do anything to get them back out there until the argument is resolved.

On the other hand, if you've self-published and you don't like a distributor, you can remove or add your books to wherever you like. You're the King/Queen! Rock on!

Along with the need to hold onto your fiction's rights, most publishers will also establish other arbitrary rules to protect themselves and maximize their profit. For example, another author that I know signed on with a traditional publisher and he already had ten novels completed. He signed away the distribution rights to the publisher and then waited for the books to show up. Unfortunately, because he was new to the world of publishing, he agreed to a contract that only allowed for two of his books to be published per year. On a personal level, he wishes that he had never made the deal. All of his fans are begging for the next book and all that he wants to do is give it to them. He doesn't care about arbitrary distribution schedules, only making his readers happy, but because he signed that contract, his hands are tied.

The biggest advantage, and the one no one ever seems to talk about, is oversight.

When I self-publish my novels, I can sign into a website (bookmarked on my phone and my computer) and tell you exactly how many books I have sold that day, month, or year with almost up-to-the-minute reporting.

Going the traditional route takes that away. Some publishers will give you monthly, quarterly, or annual sales reports but (and I'm slamming my fists as I say it) that isn't good enough.

I'll touch on it only briefly here, because there's a whole chapter up ahead that covers it, but the reason infrequent sales reporting isn't good enough is because when you publish your book, you're no longer *just* an author. You become a sales representative for your brand.

What does that even mean?

It means that your book has just become a living thing that changes daily based on who is or isn't buying it. Daily reporting of your sales numbers can show you the daily response to any sort of marketing approach that you take. If *Marketing Approach X* isn't working, then you'll know within a day and can try *Marketing Approach Y* instead, and maximize sales. Traditional publishing's sparse reporting doesn't give you that kind of feedback.

Why would you want to Self-Publish?

- You want complete ownership of your work.
- You want to make more money.
- You want complete visibility on how well your novel is selling.

Nothing Is Wrong With Traditional

As I said previously, Traditional has a lot of great aspects. Don't take what I'm saying as some sort of slam on Traditional Publishing. If a traditional publisher came up to me today and wanted to purchase the rights to one of my novels, I would at least consider it.

Traditional just isn't the path that I chose. Some folks out there, such as the famously Self-Published Hugh Howey, still take the random traditional book deal when it comes along because of some of those advantages.

Specifically, if your book is going to end up being in another language, a Traditional Book Deal will take care of the foreign work for you. I don't speak German, but if *Random Stranger* or *The Trials of Obed Marsh* were suddenly big in that country, I wouldn't know the first thing about getting my novels into those markets. A Traditional path would be very advantageous.

I keep using the phrasing "Paths" to describe the choice of Self-Published versus Traditional, but that might be the wrong word to use. Taking a path limits you to what is in front of and behind you. In the case of Hugh Howey, and several other authors that I know, you don't have to take just one path at all. Some books of yours might be better aimed toward a Traditional path while others might be better aimed at being Self-Published. It's your career and you can do whatever you want with it.

Most importantly, do what you need to do with your books to make the most of your career. There is no wrong "path."

Part 3: Getting Edited

You Don't Always Get What You Pay For

You're going to edit your story yourself, right?

Right?

You damned well better not.

Editing is a must and that goes without saying. The biggest enemy of being self-published is the handful of poorly edited products that litter the market directly next to our well-worked pieces of art. I won't say all of them, but a large number of them were edited by the author.

That's stupid.

You're not writing a book for yourself, you're writing a book for your audience. If you baked a cake, would you taste-test it? Well, yes, you probably would, but you should have someone else taste it, too. So, shouldn't you have someone else take a look at your book?

That's a horrible example followed by a rhetorical question. The answer is yes. Don't be dumb.

That being said, this is a book about not spending any money, and editing costs. The best quotes that I've seen for editing from online companies is $0.014 per word. From there the price can get upwards of almost two cents on some sites, but at $0.014 a fifty thousand word novel (NaNoWriMo sized) would cost you $700.00 to get edited.

That's hardly free.

Want to hear a secret?

You don't always get what you pay for and *Inexpensive doesn't mean 'Cheap.'*

That goes for edits as well. Many resources exist that can give you quality edits for no cost, you just need to know where to find them.

Before you go and pay those large numbers for editing, why not look at some other sources? What you really need is someone who reads a lot and doesn't mind taking a very critical look at your work.

Such as:

- **Your odd friend with a boring job and an English degree.**

You have a friend whose job is to sit in front of a computer or at a desk all day waiting for things to happen (i.e.: he or she is an e-reader salesman at a bookstore)? Ask them if they have the time and the want to read over your stuff and judge your overuse of the word "as."

- **Your spouse's coworker.**

Does your spouse have someone who really wants to help everyone around them? Can they read? Perfect! Move in for the kill!

- **Your spouse/sibling/neighbor.**

They are family and they owe you for how awesome you are. Plus this will give them the perfect list of things to point out every time they need to remind you that you aren't as awesome as you think you are.

- **Join a Writing Group.**

A Writing group is a great place to find other people with the same ambitions as you and just as much need for an editor. This gives you the rare opportunity to earn your edits through trade. Edit their documents in exchange for them editing yours. Plus, if you have a large group and a strong printer, you can hand out multiple copies of your book to different members of the group and get a large amount of feedback.

- **Websites for Authors.**

There are some websites, (WritersCafe.org is a perfect example) that allow you to post your stories (any length) in a private setting. People can then read your works and provide you with great feedback. This also has the added benefit of building hype for your story before it is released.

- **Beta Readers.**

A Beta Reader, as defined by the omniscient Wikipedia, is "a non-professional reader who reads a written work, generally fiction, with the intent of looking over the material to find and improve elements such as grammar and spelling, as well as suggestions to improve the story, its characters, or its setting." So, everyone previously mentioned in this list would be considered a Beta Reader, but my specific meaning is those found on NaNoWriMo.org. Previously in this chapter, I mentioned NaNoWriMo, and for those of you not "in the know," NaNoWriMo stands for National Novel Writing Month. It takes place during the month of November and is a sort of unofficial contest against yourself to write 50,000 words in one month. For those that are serious about the craft, it can be quite fun. Most importantly, it includes a large community of artists begging to help in every way that they can, and not only during the month of November.

NaNoWriMo.org has a forum that brings all of those artists together. One section in that forum is for posting if you need a Beta Reader. You should leverage these resources and feel free to offer your own services up. The best thing about community is cooperation.

Also, if you go onto Google and search for Beta Readers you'll find a huge community of people who just want to help you polish your prose. At first glance, there's a Beta Reader group on GoodReads and a website called Betafinder.com.

I don't think it has anything to do with fish.

As far as what I do, I'm actually a good mix of most of these options. I love using every NaNoWriMo resource that I can find and I have a great friend who does most of my edits in her spare time. I have even used my wife's coworker and a writing group.

Try everything out and find what works for you and your novel.

Part 4: Getting A Cover

Do It Yourself

I've heard a lot of people talk about designing a cover in much the same way that they say that old quote about lawyers who defend themselves.

The good news is that if you are properly prepared and you have the time and dedication to learn what you need to know, then you can go ahead and be that lawyer and defend yourself all day long.

What I'm trying to say is that there are a lot of great pay options available for designing a book cover, but you don't need to spend money if you're willing to do the legwork...

...and there is plenty of legwork.

All of that legwork won't be so difficult if you follow a very simple set of instructions:

Plan your work and then work your plan.

So, the first thing that you need to do is plan your work.

By plan your work, I mean that you need to plan how you want your cover to look and gather the tools you'll need to make your cover.

When I need to design how my cover is going to look, I grab my notebook and start doodling. They are ugly doodles, and they should be. I'm not trying to draw my cover, I'm just sketching out where the ideas are going to go that I want in my final design. For example, when Robert Reynolds and I were designing the cover to our young adult fantasy novel, *The Sons of Merlin*, we knew that the central weapon of the story, Excalibur, should feature prominently in the cover. So, we took out our notepads and started scribbling ideas with a sword in them.

You know the best part about our scribbles?

The sword was a poorly drawn cross in most of them. Just a scribble with other stuff directly around it. We knew another huge idea of the book that we wanted on the cover was the dichotomy of good versus evil that is prominent in the book.

How did we handle that?

In one case we draw the "sword" scribble down the middle of the page and put a circle on each side. In the circle on the left we wrote down ideas for dark and evil, and in the circle on the right we wrote down ideas for light and good.

We had a basic plan, and from there we needed to gather the tools.

The tools started with the proper images. You're going to need the images that you think fit in those locations. The best sources that I've found for free stock photos are Wikimedia Commons (commons.wikimedia.org) and Unsplash (unsplash.com).

Wikimedia has a large database of everything from images to sound clips that you can use in all of your works. My favorite part of Wikimedia is the ability to search engine (something that Unsplash lacks).

Unsplash on the other hand has a large collection of high resolution stock images that consist largely of landscapes but not only landscapes. They are high quality images, which can't be said for everything on Wikimedia. The cover of this book is actually made from an image off of Unsplash.

There are other great websites you can use, you only have to Google search for the words "Free Stock Photos."

In the case of *The Sons of Merlin*, Bob and I had narrowed the light and dark argument down to landscapes. We wanted a dark landscape that turns into a light landscape with the sword as a border.

To shorten our personal story up, we found our three images (a sword and two landscapes) on Wikimedia Commons after days of combing through images. We even found an image of a jewel to add to the sword, making it even more "magical."

Now you need the rest of your tools, and that means the program that will help you piece them all together.

A lot of you are thinking I'm about to say Photoshop, and you are completely wrong.

Alright, well maybe not completely, but close enough. You want something *like* Photoshop, because Photoshop costs money and we are trying to do this whole process on a budget.

What you really want is GIMP (www.gimp.org). GIMP is an open source program that is essentially the same as Photoshop.

Right about now, you're starting to freak out. You don't know Photoshop, why the hell should you know GIMP?

It's ok. Take a deep breath.

I could sit here and type out a very in-depth tutorial on how to use GIMP or any other service in this book, but I wouldn't be able to do it the justice that it would deserve. Besides, there are so many better tutorials out on Youtube than I could do for you.

That being said, go to Youtube and look up Elisabeth Niederhut's video, "How To Make A Book Cover for Createspace Using GIMP." If you don't have a Createspace account, go ahead and create one during this tutorial. You're going to need it later in this book.

Elisabeth Niederhut is a self-publisher as well, and her video is a great step-by-step tutorial on creating your own cover.

Right about now, half of you are freaking out again because you only want to do an e-book and don't think you need a full cover with backing.

Calm down. You can still use this tutorial for two reasons.

The first reason is that you can easily just cut the picture in half and "Abra Kadabra" you have an e-book cover. Certain sites require that it be a specific size in pixels so go into your image properties and adjust it until it's the right size.

The second reason is that yes, you will need a full cover, because, as I will show you later in this book, it costs you nothing to have a physical book out there making sales of you as well. So, why wouldn't you have a full cover?

There's also a small selection of you that will be writing just short stories only meant to be in electronic format. More power to you. Just stick with the first reason and you can make all the e-book covers you like.

Another great tool to use is Pixlr Editor (http://apps.pixlr.com/editor/). Pixlr Editor is a tool that is very similar to GIMP or Photoshop in the available toolbox and in the layout. The difference is that it's accessible through a web browser without any download. You can use it in the exact same way that you would use GIMP, but if you're like me and prefer to type your stories on a Chromebook or other web-based platform, then you're out of luck with GIMP and Photoshop.

One thing to note about Pixlr, though, is that because it's web-based, it has a tendency to crash. You can avoid this ruining your life if you just remember to save the project regularly.

That should just be a rule in your life: Save your projects regularly.

Once again, I'm not going to give you a full tutorial on how to use Pixlr Editor when so many exist already that would be so much better than anything that I could produce for you.

Instead, swing on over to Youtube (again) and search for "How to Make a Wattpad Cover on Pixlr Tutorial" by 'marvelous_'. It's a basic tutorial to help you familiarize yourself with the tools, and to also give you an end result book cover. Wattpad is a great tool for authors as well, and I encourage you to check it out, but that's not really why you should watch the video. Wattpad's covers are just like every other e-book website's covers and the tutorial will help you with all of them.

If you're doing a Createspace cover and still want to use Pixlr Editor, go ahead and watch both videos, as the first translates well into the second.

Have Someone Else DIY

Wow, that's a lot of work, and I'm not just saying that because of how beautifully simple it is to segue into this chapter. I've made all of my own covers, and some other book covers for friends and clients, and each cover has been a pain in the butt every time.

Even if I finish the first cover and I like the way it looks, that doesn't mean that I've followed all of Createspace or whoever's guidelines accurately.

Nothing is more frustrating than relaxing with a beer after you've just submitted the cover of your dreams to Createspace and then finding out about 12 hours later that it didn't meet their requirements for "insert a random vague reference here."

Well, almost nothing. If I had just completed my manuscript, hadn't backed it up, and my computer died, I would probably kill myself.

I digress.

Some people (read that "most people") do not have the patience to sit through two Youtube videos, search for stock photos, learn GIMP or Pixlr Editor, and then risk rejection from Createspace.

That's only half of it.

The image you produce in this fashion isn't going to be anything like the one in your head, unless you're a well-practiced graphic artist. This could be for a lot of reasons. You might have an image in your head about a man riding his horse through a snow covered field while roping a calf.

Now go find those free stock photos.

In short, you either won't or you won't have the skills necessary to merge an image of a rope, a snow-covered field, a man sitting on a random object, and a horse together.

And why should you? You're a writer, not a graphic artist. (Unless you are a graphic artist as well. In which case, good job!)

The good news is that you don't actually have to do the work. My favorite resource for work on my novel is always going to be community, and the best community for writers helping writers is Nanowrimo.org.

Their forum is the best place to ask for help. Earlier I mentioned asking the forum for help with beta readers and editors, but it doesn't have to stop there. The NaNoWriMo forums has a subforum called "Nano Artisans" and is the best place to ask for any sort of artwork for your novel. You can ask for help with cover art, sketches of your characters, and logos. It's a community that wants to help you visualize your dream.

A similar resource would be Reddit.com's different subreddits. Find one that fits your genre and ask if anyone would be willing to help you whip up a cover. It never hurts to ask.

The final thing to mention is that Createspace's Cover Creator also offers very basic cover art generation. Along with Createspace, most of the other e-book and publishing sites also have something similar. Those covers won't be drop-dead gorgeous and won't grab everyone's attention, but they'll get the job done.

Out of all of these, if you're not going to or can't do it yourself, I recommend checking out the NaNoWriMo forum.

Sometimes You Do Get What You Pay For

I have given you my two favorite options. In a book called "Self-Publish Without Spending Money," I have done my part and shown you the roads that I took to produce cover art that didn't cost a dime.

Unfortunately, you may not like anything that you produce graphically. You may not like anything that those wonderful people on the NaNoWriMo forums produce. This is all highly possible.

The good news is that I have already done my part and told you about the free options that I choose every time. Those were the free options that I still encourage. That's good news, because now that I have done my job, I'll give you a few paid resources that everyone seems to enjoy.

Several friends of mine are fans of Fiverr.com. Fiverr is a very unique site in that people offer their services (a ton of different types of servers for authors and writers) for only five dollars. Need a cover designed? Only five dollars. Need a book trailer? Only five dollars. Need advertising? Only five dollars.

Of course, that's usually just an introductory price and if you end up needing more, then you'll have to pay more, but five dollars for the book cover of your dreams sounds totally worth it.

Another great site that I hear a lot about, but have not yet used, is 99designs.com. From what I understand of this site, you purchase a package and tell them what kind of design you want, then artists compete for your design. You end up with an entire collection of designs to choose the one you want from and if you don't like any of them, then you don't pay. It sounds like a great way to get exactly what you want for an understandable cost. (As of this writing, the basic package is under $300).

Another great option is to put out your work to the local community. Where I live, we have several nearby colleges whose students would be a willing participant in a paid cover design. Plus, a lot of artists cruise Craigslist.com for gigs and a negotiated cover art could be one of them.

Of course, I still recommend taking the time to learn GIMP or investing your time in the NaNoWriMo community, but I won't hate you if you decided to go the Fiverr or 99Designs route.

Part 5: The Publishing Part

Kindle (With Pictures!)

Assuming that you have a finished manuscript, completed edits, and a cover that doesn't make you cringe, then it's time to send your book out to the masses.

Currently, the best market for e-books is the Kindle. Of course, it's not the only market, and I will have an entire section on getting your book on the other e-readers as well. I'm a firm believer in putting your book in as many venues as possible.

The website you need to head to is http://kdp.amazon.com. The KDP part of the address stands for Kindle Direct Publishing. Kindle Direct Publishing is where you add books to the Kindle e-reader and where you will see your marketing and sales stats. It's also a place where you will get most of your questions on publishing answered in the KDP Community forums.

Once you create an account and sign in to KDP, you will want to click "Add new title."

Once you click "Add new title," it will take you to a page where you can fill in all of the details regarding your book. The first section of this page is asking for you to sign up for KDP Select. Read it thoroughly. If you decide that you want to do KDP Select, you can go ahead and ignore the section of this book that includes putting your book in other stores. KDP Select trades you perks such as marketing and promotional benefits in exchange for keeping your book only in their store and nowhere else.

At the time of this writing, I personally don't find the perks of KDP Select to be worth the exclusivity that goes along with it. That's a decision for you.

Step 1 **Your book** ✓ Not Started.	Step 2 **Rights & Pricing** ✓ Not Started.	Optional **KDP Select Benefits**

Introducing KDP Select

Take advantage of KDP Select, an optional program that makes your book exclusive to Kindle and eligible for the following benefits:

- **Reach more readers** – With each 90-day enrollment period, your book will appear in the Kindle Owners' Lending Library (KOLL) and reach the growing number of Amazon Prime customers in the U.S., U.K., Germany, France, and Japan.
- **Earn more money** – Every time your book is borrowed from KOLL, you'll earn your share of the monthly KDP Select Global Fund. You can also earn a 70% royalty for sales to customers in Japan, Brazil, India and Mexico.
- **Maximize your sales potential** – Choose from two promotional tools including: Kindle Countdown Deals, time-bound promotional discounts for your book, available on Amazon.com and Amazon.co.uk, while earning royalties; or Free Book Promotion, where readers can get your book free for a limited time.

Learn more

☐ **Enroll this book in KDP Select**

By checking this box, you are enrolling in KDP Select for 90 days. Books enrolled in KDP Select must not be available in digital format on any other platform during their enrollment. If your book is found to be available elsewhere in digital format, it may not be eligible to remain in the program. See the KDP Select Terms and Conditions and KDP Select FAQs for more information.

FAQs

Who are contributors?
Contributors are the people involved in creating your book. You can identify your book's author, editor, illustrator, translator, and more. To publish your book, at least one contributor name is required, and all contributors of any public domain content are required. Enter contributor names in the order in which you want them to appear in the Kindle store

Should I use my physical book's ISBN?
Do not use an ISBN from a print edition for your digital edition. If you want to include an ISBN for the digital version of your book, it must be a unique ISBN. Learn more

Whichever decision you make, your mother and I will still love you.

The next section includes really simple questions that I hope you have already answered long before this, such as Title, Subtitle (if you have one), and Editions (Optional). There's also a section asking you the publisher's name. You can either leave this blank or put your name in there.

1. Enter Your Book Details

Book name

> The Early Adventures of Andrew Doran

Please enter the exact title only. Books submitted with extra words in this field will not be published. (Why?)

Subtitle (optional)

Please enter the exact subtitle only. Books submitted with extra words in this field will not be published. (Why?)

☐ This book is part of a series (What's this?)

Edition number (optional) (What's this?)

Publisher (optional) (What's this?)

Description (What's this?)

> What led him down the path toward defending humanity? What does a boy in the early 1920's do when his entire world is turned upside down by the sudden intrusion of spirits and monsters?
> This is the tale of the beginning of Andrew Doran.

3675 characters left

Also in this space is your description for your book. Take your time writing the description. These will be the words that capture your readers and convince them to buy your book.

If you would like to make your description pop out, you could always add some of the html codes that are approved by Amazon. I would like to put an emphasis on the word 'some.' With html in descriptions, less is more.

The Amazon approved list for acceptable html tags is:

HTML Tag	Description
`<b>`	Formats enclosed text as bold.
` `	Creates a line break.
`<em>`	Emphasizes the enclosed text; generally formatted as italic.
`<font>`	Determines the appearance of the enclosed text.
`<h1>` to `<h6>`	Formats enclosed text as a section heading: `<h1>` (largest) through `<h6>` (smallest).
`<hr>`	Creates a horizontal "rule" or line. Often used to divide sections of text.
`<i>`	Formats enclosed text as italic.
`<li>`	Identifies an item in an ordered (numbered) or unordered (bulleted) list.
`<ol>`	Creates a numbered list from enclosed items, each of which is identified by a `<li>` tag.
`<p>`	Defines a paragraph of text with the first line indented; creates a line break at the end of the enclosed text.
`<pre>`	Defines preformatted text.
`<s>`	Formats text as ~~strikethrough~~. See also, `<strike>`.
`<strike>`	Formats text as ~~strikethrough~~. See also, `<s>`.
`<strong>`	Formats enclosed text as bold. See also, `<b>`.
`<sub>`	Formats enclosed text as subscript: reduces the font size and drops it below the baseline.
`<sup>`	Formats enclosed text as superscript: reduces the font

\>   size and places it above the baseline.

    \<u\>   Formats enclosed text as <u>underlined</u>.

    \<ul\>   Creates a bulleted list from enclosed items, each of which is identified by a \<li\> tag.

Close any html tag that you start by adding a slash (ie: if it starts \<b\> end the sentence with \</b\>).

When you've finished making your book description as pretty as a skunk under your boss' car, the next button that you will want to click is Book Contributors.

This is where you add who the author is (presumably you) and where you'll also add any editors, cover designers, co-authors, or uncles to your book. This is a required step, but the only required part is that you need an author. Adding any other contributors is completely optional.

Next, you'll choose the language that your book is written in and the publication date (presumably today's date if this is the first time that you've done this).

The next optional box is going to be a request for you to input any ISBN's that you have. ISBNs are a 13 digit numerical identifier for recognizing your book nationally. It stands for International Standard Book Number.

This optional box is here mostly to confuse you. ISBN's are provided for free from each of the self-publishing vendors. Kindle books are put under their own type of ISBN, called an ASIN. You don't need to go and spend money on an ISBN, ever. If you already have an ISBN, probably provided by a traditional publisher, or that you went ahead and purchased without consulting with me first, this is where you would enter it.

Don't buy an ISBN. Amazon, Barnes and Noble, Kobo, and the rest all assign you unique identifiers for your work. You will never need an ISBN. When you're on the Createspace site, you might argue differently, but when it comes to e-books you should be completely fine without one.

Note: The comment about ISBN's in Createspace is only if you would prefer to be listed as the publisher instead of Createspace. For most people, that kind of detail doesn't matter, but for some people it does and that's entirely up to you.

The next step is to verify your publishing rights. If you wrote the story, it is completely yours. Public Domain works are works that have no copyright on them and anyone can do anything they want with. If you wrote your book, it is 100% yours, so go ahead and claim it by selecting the "This is not a public domain work and I hold the necessary publishing rights."

2. Verify Your Publishing Rights

Verify Your Publishing Rights (What's this?)

○ This is a public domain work.

◉ This is not a public domain work and I hold the necessary publishing rights.

The selection of your book's genre usually sounds easier than it is. I always have a great idea of what my book's genre is until I see the humongous list that Amazon provides for labeling your books. The next section is that choice. You can choose two identifiers for your book. If it is action and adventure with a touch of the paranormal, be certain to put it under both Action and Adventure, and the Paranormal designations.

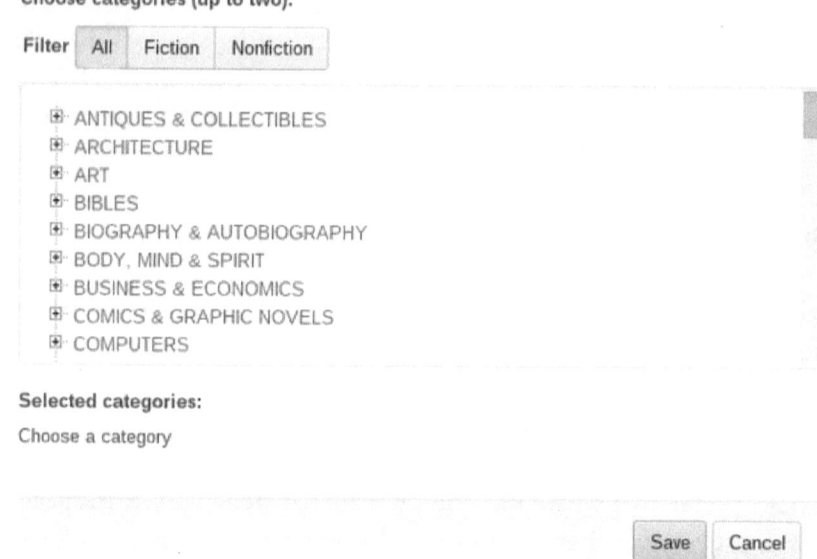

Remember that book cover that you didn't pay someone to make? Section 4 is where you add that.

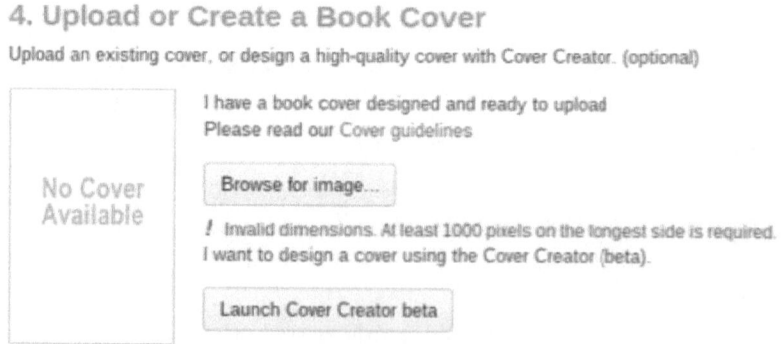

The image here shows you that you need specific dimensions for your cover. This is another great example of how important a program like GIMP or Pixlr Editor is. In both of those you can set the dimensions of your image. Unfortunately, you're going to become very familiar with this feature. Each different site has a different requirement for the pixel size of their covers. It can be frustrating and some days you might want to pull your hair out because of it. My suggestion is to shave your head and keep on working.

The "Cover Creator Beta" is a great tool if you don't want to spend too much time worrying about your cover. This is the same thing that I was saying about the Createspace Cover Creator tool (essentially the same since they are both Amazon). It will serve well to give you a basic cover that also looks professional.

The fifth section is where you will upload your book file. Amazon accepts .doc, .docx, .pdf, and .mobi formats.

5. Upload Your Book File

Select a digital rights management (DRM) option: [What's this?]

○ Enable digital rights management

◉ Do not enable digital rights management

Book content file:

Browse

This is also the section in which you will be selecting whether you would like your book to be protected with digital rights management, or DRM. DRM protects your book from being used in other platforms or transferred to another user's account. It's meant to stop piracy, but the state of piracy in the world allows for plenty of resources to make your book available anyway.

There is also a marketing approach that assumes that DRM protected books actually sell incredibly less than books that don't use DRM. I'll leave you to do your own research as my own personal experiments are far from over in that regard.

Once your book is uploaded, the Amazon system will examine your file for spelling errors. It's practically useless for actual edits, so don't use it that way, but it is helpful to see if anything in your document is so ridiculous that KDP caught it. For example, it showed me that in my horror novel, *The Trials of Obed Marsh*, the thirty times that I used the word 'fishmen' were hyphenated. I had originally intended not to hyphenate them and of course this needed to be corrected.

I mean, 'fish-men' looks so much sillier than 'fishmen.' Am I right?

With your document uploaded, you can now preview how it's going to look on the kindle e-reader. If you think it looks beautiful, go ahead and hit 'Save and Continue.'

If you don't like it, make the necessary adjustments and upload it again. There's no limit to how many times you can upload it.

✓ Upload and conversion successful!

✓ Spell Check
There are 0 possible spelling errors.

6. Preview Your Book

Previewing your book is an integral part of the publishing process and the best way to guarantee that your readers will have a good experience and see the book you want them to see. KDP offers two options to preview your book depending on your needs. Which should I use?

Online Previewer

For most users, the online previewer is the best and easiest way to preview your content. The online previewer allows you to preview most books as they will appear on Kindle, Kindle Fire, iPad, and iPhone. If your book is fixed layout (for more information on fixed layout, see the Kindle Publishing Guidelines), the online previewer will display your book as it will appear on Kindle Fire.

Preview book

Downloadable Previewer

If you would like to preview your book on Kindle Touch or Kindle DX, you will want to use the downloadable previewer.

Instructions
> Download Book Preview File
> Download HTML
> Download Previewer:
  Windows | Mac

The second page is about Rights and Pricing of your novel and the first section covers your rights.

Step 1	Step 2
Your book	**Rights & Pricing**
✓ Complete	ⓘ Not Started...

7. Verify Your Publishing Territories

Select the territories for which you hold rights: (What's this?)

- ◉ Worldwide rights - all territories
- ○ Individual territories - select territories

Select: All | None

United States
United Kingdom
Guernsey
Isle Of Man
Jersey
Canada

Selected territories (0 of 245)

In short, if you wrote an original work, then you own it everywhere and can select 'Worldwide rights.'

You will choose your royalties and price next. Of course, you're going to want to have a 70% royalty, but that isn't always the case. The limitations are based on how much you charge and where you charge it. Certain locations don't allow for 70% royalty if you haven't selected KDP Select. Also, if your book is less than $2.99 you can only charge 35%.

Pricing is more than "How much can I make?" More importantly, pricing is a marketing tool. A lot of people prefer to put the first book in their series (if you're writing a series) at a lower price. This gets people hooked and if they like your book they'll buy the next one at a marked up price.

Smashwords, another site to publish books, did a study on how many books sell at what price points and the majority of books that sell are priced between $2.99 and $3.99, blowing away the less-than-a-dollar price points.

This is where you decide the price that you want for your book and there are a lot of factors to take into consideration.

How long is your book?

How long did your book take to write?

What prices are books of similar length and genre being charged for online?

These are only some of the things that you should be paying attention to when you choose your price.

Finally, you'll have the options for Kindle Matchbook and Kindle Lending.

If you opt into Kindle Matchbook, people who buy your paperback version of your book will be able to get your e-book at a discounted or free price option.

If you opt into the Kindle Lending, it means that if someone buys your book, they can share it with their Kindle friends for a limited time.

Check the box confirming that you own all of the rights and are ready to publish and then hit "Save and Publish."

Now, just wait about 12 hours, and your book should pop up in the Kindle store!

You're now published, and you didn't have to spend a dime!

Everywhere Else

Kindle might be the current big game in town for publishing your e-books, but they aren't the only game. Besides, you don't want to be published in only one store or format. The wider you spread your net, the more fish you will gather.

Draft2Digital:

I put Draft2Digital on here, instead of Smashwords, because it's just easier. Both are distribution sites that will put your e-books on every other e-reader out there, but Smashwords has incredibly stringent formatting rules and regulations. Smashwords also seems to take longer (in my personal experience) in getting your books onto those other sites. Unfortunately, Smashwords also has one of the better marketing tools: Coupon Codes. They allow you to set specific prices and have deals for permanent or set periods of time.

Draft2Digital, though, will create a Createspace print file for you that you can use when making your print book, and that's something that, as of this book's publication date, Smashwords can't do.

Head on over to Draft2Digital.com and create a log in. Once that's done, make sure that you're on the page "My Books."

On that page, there's a huge orange button labeled "Add New Book."

Go ahead and click that.

This takes you to an "Edit Book" page. While the layout is kind of different, it's essentially all of the same information that you gave when you were making your Kindle formatted version.

You will upload your book file, fill out the title information, and ignore the ISBN. BISAC information at the end is just referring to which genre you think your book falls into.

The second page takes you to a place where you'll upload your cover and make sure that the chapter headings match. If they don't match, go ahead and try to change them yourself or send them a quick message explaining the issue. I had a small issue with none of my chapters showing correctly and after I sent them a quick message they had fixed it within 24 hours. Your results may vary.

The next page is Preview Book Layout. This page is the part that impresses me the most. Here, you can download a Createspace (print ready) version of your manuscript, with page numbers and properly formatted for the Createspace machinery.

Honestly, I don't know how I survived before I discovered this nifty tool. It cuts your publishing time almost in half.

Download the Createspace file, click that you've reviewed your document (after, of course, you've reviewed your document) and then move to the next screen.

This screen is where you'll set the price of your book. Go ahead and select all of the markets that you want to publish to, and then click the big, orange Submit button.

Clicking submit brings up a new popup that asks if the book is yours and if you are ready to publish. Click that you own the works and then submit it.

Success!

From here, you can work through Draft2Digital to make a Createspace (paperback) version of your book, but I haven't done Createspace through Draft2Digital, and have always opted to manage that process myself.

Createspace:

Createspace is where you'll make the paperback version of your book. A lot of people have different places they'd like you to go: Lulu.com, Lightning Source, Tate Publishing, or whatever. I choose the Createspace route, not because the others are bad, but because Createspace is simple and has free expanded distribution.

Expanded distribution is what gets your books into every store possible. When you're done putting all of your files together, selecting Createspace expanded distribution will allow people to order your physical book at stores like Barnes and Noble or a million different places online.

Sign up for a Createspace log in if you haven't already. I will give you a brief walkthrough on how to publish a book to Createspace, but just in case, be sure to check out Workersonboard's youtube video, "How to Publish and Sell your Book on Createspace," https://www.youtube.com/watch?v=ihvTqd_pafw .

Createspace has a guided process that helps you through the entire creation of your novels.

A lot of this will be similar to what you had to do for your Kindle version of your book. The Title information should be identical to your Kindle formatted version, and I kind of hinted at what would be happening with the ISBN.

You will be completely fine with the Createspace-supplied free ISBN unless having Createspace as the publisher for your book is somehow offensive to you.

The Interior section is where you'll upload that file that we downloaded previously from Draft2digital.com. Once it's uploaded, it will take a while to review the file. It will then have you inspect it, claiming that there are errors of some sort. That's for you to judge. My errors are usually regarding the DPI quality in my author image and that the document was off in size. Both errors it automatically will correct or ignore, but if you have any other issues go ahead and edit your file and attempt to upload it again.

The cover, again. This is the point in which you'll be happy I suggested you shave your head earlier. The cover creator is very specific in that you can't go beyond trim borders. Otherwise, go ahead and upload the cover you worked on previously. Once you've launched the cover creator, it will walk you through a step-by-step process of preparing your cover for print. If things don't happen to fit, go ahead and open up GIMP or Pixlr Editor and make the necessary changes and upload it again.

Once the Interior and Cover sections are completed, it's just a matter of sending your files in for review.

They like to give you a warning that your files will take between 24 and 48 hours to be reviewed. In my practice, I've never had to wait more than 12 hours for a response. Of their responses, they are very good at telling you exactly which element had the issue, but not always what the issue was. For example, they will tell you that your cover has elements that run over the trim-line, but they won't ever tell you which elements. My suggestion here is to assume that it's all of your elements and pull everything back a little further from the trim-line.

When you finally get your book approved by the file review people in the sky, they'll ask you to proof your book. Normally, companies make you pay to have the proof printed and sent to you so that you can review it and then approve it.

That won't be necessary, because Createspace gives you a pdf copy of the proof. It's the same proof that they use to make the print version that they would have sent to you, so go ahead and download and review that. The pdf is completely free, and is what you would have received if you had ordered the book anyway.

When you finish reviewing your proof, if you like what you see, go ahead and hit the Approve button.

If you don't like what you see, you will need to go back and make whatever necessary changes you've decided need to make and re-upload your manuscript.

Word of warning, whatever changes you might make to the way the story is typed should be duplicated in the e-book versions. So, if you found something like a misspelling and need it corrected, you should go back and correct it in every version of your book. Just to be thorough.

Part 6: Sales Is A Good Word

Sales Is Not Marketing

There are a lot of negative stigmas associated with the word "Sales."

I don't like that.

I was listening to an interview with actor and former Fourth Doctor from the famous television series "Doctor Who," Tom Baker, when he said something that I felt fit perfectly.

I'm paraphrasing, but he said, "Everything is seduction. You seduce an employer to hire you and you seduce a new acquaintance into being your friend."

My quote isn't exact. As a matter of fact, I'm probably even remembering it wrong, except for the part "Everything is seduction." He definitely said that.

I digress. My point is that your audience is only going to buy from someone they like, so seduce them. That's what sales is.

If I'm a printer salesman, I'm going to walk into a business, any business, and I'm not going to walk up to the secretary's desk and say "Hey, wanna buy a printer?"

That doesn't sell anything, at all.

Instead, I'm going to walk up to the secretary's desk, and say something like, "Hi," I'll take my hat off and gently stick out my hand for a shake. "My name is Matt. How are you today?"

That's two sentences and I've said nothing about printers. Why? Because, even though it's just small talk, it's endearing. I'm demonstrating that I'm someone who actually wants to know how his or her day is going.

I'm not being overly aggressive, I'm just being polite. The secretary knows that I'm there for some sort of business reason, but already he or she is more inclined to talk to me, just because I've disarmed them by being pleasant.

I've seduced them.

Of course, this is a staged example, but try it in a book environment.

At your next book signing (or possibly your first, so, good luck!), don't be the author that sits behind the table and waits for someone to engage them, but also don't be the author who is shouting "Buy my book, please!"

Instead, just greet everyone who walks within five feet of your table. If you're feeling gutsy, walk around and introduce yourself.

I spent 3 years selling those e-readers that I mentioned at the beginning of this book, and while I was a trapped victim for the chatty people, I actually had them just as trapped in my web. My e-reader booth was set up directly in front of the door to the store, so I greeted anyone who came in with a very bright and sincere smile, a hello, and followed it up with a "How is your day going?" Somewhere around sixty percent of the time, people would just ignore me or nod as a means of acknowledging me. The rest of the time, they engaged me. They said hi back, or discussed their drive in. We began discussing other things, and I would find a way to turn it back toward the device that I was trying to sell.

That works at your hypothetical book signing as well. You've made your greetings, you've asked them how they are doing, they feel obliged to ask you how you're doing and you can easily spin it toward your books.

For example:

"I'm doing alright. How are you doing?" asks the random stranger walking by your table.

"Me? I'm doing wonderful. I just accomplished my dream come true and became a published author," you answer with pride and gusto!

Now the random stranger walking by your table is inclined to ask you about your book or figuratively applaud your accomplishment.

The point that I'm trying to make is that you need to engage people to succeed at making sales. I have seen authors sitting at their booths and playing on their iPads and never engaging a single person. Those same authors, hours later, were complaining because they didn't sell a single book, but sitting directly next to them was an author with a mediocre book cover and a plot that didn't sound overly exciting and he sold out of his books. The difference was that while the first author was playing Angry Chimpanzees on his iPad, the second author was having conversations with anyone who would give him the time of day.

If you engage your audience, they will give you their time, and time really is money.

That's what sales are.

Sales is not Marketing, though.

What I mean by that is, if someone asks you if you've been selling your book and you answer that you sent out thirty tweets, forty Facebook posts, and a picture of yourself writing the next great novel on Instagram, then you're not answering the original question.

Instead, all of those are marketing tactics. Marketing is putting print or copy in front of your audience so that they will glance at it and think about your product. All of this is with the hope that your marketing tactics will bring in new buyers. You need to market, but marketing is not selling.

Selling, as you might have pulled from the examples above, is convincing someone to buy your book. You're not convincing someone to buy your book with a Facebook post or tweet. At best, you're letting them know that your book exists and they might decide, on their own, that that's something they would like to spend their money on.

Selling is telling someone that your book exists and then sharing with them the value of why that book belongs in their hands. You don't want them deciding that they might take a chance on your book, you want them wondering how they ever lived without it.

That's the difference between sales and marketing.

Both are very important, but a lot of authors are very good at marketing, and so few are very good at selling.

All you need to remember about selling your book is to engage your audience. If you engage your audience in a personal and non-aggressive manner, the sale will happen naturally. Customers would rather buy from friends than a salesman. So, don't be a salesman, be their friend and the sale will follow.

#1 Rule Of Sales: Activity Breeds Success

The title of this chapter is the mantra that almost every successful salesman has. I work in sales (if you couldn't tell) and two of my closer coworkers both repeat this to me daily. They say it differently, but they always say it.

It's a very simple math equation that means the more people you engage, the more sales you will have. Success is guaranteed.

I'll break it down just a little further for you. If I start sending out a newsletter to my reader-base whenever I have a new deal on my books, and I know that 30% of the people who I mail the newsletter to will open it, and only 2% of the entire list will actually buy something, I can make some simple, yet accurate assumptions.

If we assign those percentages all numbers, we can form a game plan.

Say that my list only has 100 people signed up for it. I go ahead and I send out my newsletter that *Andrew Doran at the Mountains of Madness* is on sale, this weekend only. Based on my percentages, I know that 30 out of my 100 people subscribed to my newsletter will actually read it. From that, I also know that only 2 people will buy it.

Sending a newsletter to 100 people resulted in me getting two sales.

If I believe that #1 rule of sale, and that activity breeds success, I know that I need to increase my activity. I need more people subscribed to my newsletter.

At the next three signings I ask anyone who walks by my table if they would be interested in hearing more about my books. Anyone who says yes and gives me their email address gets added to my newsletter mailing list.

At the end of those three signings, I have 200 people total on my list.

By the previous numbers, I know that I just doubled my book sales per newsletter. Instead of only two people acting on my next big promotion, I now have four verified purchases every time I send out the newsletter.

This can be stretched to include any face-to-face sales event as well. Remember earlier when I used the two authors to illustrate how to engage your audience? The guy on his iPad had absolutely no activity and he saw no success. The second author, sitting at the table next to him engaged everyone who came to his table.

He was a hive of activity and as a result he saw a lot of success.

Your novel is your baby, and your writing is your career. Both are things that you should be proud to tell the world about. Tell everyone about your books. The grocer, the barber, the candlestick maker, whoever!

The more people that you engage, the more sales you will make. Simple.

#2 Rule Of Sales: Avoid Insanity

Another rule of sales is to avoid insanity. By insanity, I'm specifically referencing the famous quote that defines the word insanity as "doing the same thing over and over again and expecting different results."

If you haven't sold any books in the last three months, but you haven't changed your approach to selling books, then your fourth month isn't going to be any different. You can only blame the book market so much. In the end, your book sales are determined by how well you can grab your audience, and if the things that you're doing to grab your audience aren't working, you must reevaluate them and try something completely different.

For example, if I went ahead and made the first book in my first series completely free and saw a huge sales boon in the rest of that series, I might think that I should do the same thing with each of my series.

So, in month two, I take my second series and do the same thing, making the first book free but not the rest.

Unexpectedly, I don't see anywhere near the results that I had the first time around.

Well, maybe that was a fluke. I'll try it again on month three.

Month three was more like month two than month one and I find myself confused.

This is when I need to reevaluate my strategy. Whatever had made the first series sell so well hadn't infected my other series. It's time for something new, maybe instead of giving away the first book in the series to everyone for free, I could just limit the free copies to people who subscribed to the newsletter. Or maybe I could make the last book in the series free? Or sell the first book with a complimentary banana?

The point is to keep your strategies fluid. You can't make sales if you're not prepared to evolve your strategies with how the market reacts.

Avoid doing the same thing over and over again and expecting different results.

Part 7: Marketing

Get Legitimate Reviews

There are a lot of ways to market, and you should be using them all (that's part of that activity thing, again). I will be going into a short explanation about the major handful that you should be using in the next section.

This section is a mild PSA on reviews.

Unfortunately, there are a group of people out there that have sensed the severe need of authors such as us for reviews, and they've offered their services as reviewers...

...at a cost.

When you ask someone for a review, you want to be seen as a legitimate and honest author with a career that is noted for its integrity. The moment that you start paying for reviews, you have given up that integrity.

I know, I know. That's quite the righteous stand, but it comes from a very logical point of view. The real reason you don't buy reviews is because someone will always find out.

It sounds like paranoia, but it isn't. That's just fact. Don't believe me? Go to Google.com and search for "fake book reviews."

There are plenty of ways to get legitimate reviews. Legitimate is key. You have to take all of the reviews, both good and bad. The moment you start asking people to give you good reviews instead of honest is another time that you threaten the integrity of your work and your audience.

Before we move to the next section of this book, I would like to share the idea of using Advanced Reader Copies to get honest reviews.

A great use of marketing is to offer free copies of your books to people willing to give you reviews. In the world of Traditional Publishing, these are called Advanced Reader Copies, or ARC's. As a matter of fact, they can still be called ARC's in the self-publishing world thanks to sites like Netgalley.com. Netgalley.com is a site that has been offering Advanced Reader Copies of e-books to people who sign up. The people who sign up for Netgalley usually work for book stores or are in the book industry.

The idea behind ARC's is that you give people early (usually not final manuscripts) copies of your book in the hopes that they will give you reviews. These reviews show up before the book is actually for sale to help drive interest in your work.

As a self-published author, there are many ways to go about doing your own ARC program, aside from the Netgalley option. You can make it part of a newsletter announcing your book, you can go to social sites such as Twitter, Facebook, and Reddit, or you can ask people that you know outside of the internet.

This is a great way to generate reviews and is completely free to you.

Leveraging Your Resources

Wow, there are so many means of marketing your work. Honestly, there are almost too many, but I will try to give you a breakdown of the most important options.

Facebook:

Let's start with the first one everybody thinks that they need. Facebook is a great place to say hi to your far-away family or post pictures of that new hat that you're thinking of buying. Your family and friends do not want to be spammed with your new book (although a phone call or personalized email to your friends and family about your book would not be out of the question).

Counter to that strategy, though, you could create a Facebook page for yourself as an author. Using that page, you could invite people from other groups to like your page. The people that like your page are going to be fodder for whatever information that you put up on your page. You can talk about events that you're going to be at or new releases that you just published.

Be careful not to fall into the spamming trap, though. People will want to have a reason to come to your page, and if you are only ever posting "buy my book," over and over again, you're going to lose people quicker than you can get them to like your page. Mix it up, engage your audience, and have fun with it before sprinkling in the news about your book.

Twitter:

It's a trap!

No, not really, but it can be. When you use Twitter, try to remember what I just said for Facebook: Mix it up. It is way too easy to spam on Twitter. Take the time to ReTweet people's posts and follow people that you are genuinely interested in. When you show interest in others, they'll show interest in you. Once you get a good sized following, start tweeting, maybe only once or twice a day, about your book. The trick to Tweeting and being seen is using hashtags.

Hashtags (formerly known as the "number" or "pound sign") are labels that you give your Tweet that make it searchable. If I post a hashtag that I am an indie author (it would look like #indieauthor), anytime that someone searches for indie authors, my tweet will pop up.

Popular hashtags include:

#RT = Post this to encourage others to ReTweet your Tweet.

#amwriting = lets your fans know that you're busy writing, and for some reason people love this tag.

#amediting = same as the previous one, except...well...editing.

#authors = some of these are self-explanatory.

#books = like this one.

#deals = people looking for deals will find you.

#free = if your book is free, this hashtag will bring it to the attention of a lot of people.

That's just a few of them. Use them and remember that Twitter is a give and take relationship. You will get out of it whatever you put into it.

Goodreads:

Goodreads is my favorite type of social network. You friend people and share all of your book love. It's a lot of fun.

Even better is when you are an author on Goodreads. Once your book is published, you need to go to Goodreads.com and set up an author's page. Don't skimp on anything at all. You need a full biography and picture. Once your page is set up, the fun begins. Your readers can ask you questions and engage you in so many ways, but that's not the best part.

The best part is that you can see who adds your book to their individual "To-Read" shelves. A "To-Read" shelf is a place where people store books that they thought were interesting. It's like the queue on your Netflix. You thought it looked kind of neat, but putting it on your queue doesn't mean that you're actually going to watch it. That's the same for the Goodreads "To-Read" shelf.

Here comes that word again: Engage.

You can see a full list of everyone interested in your books, so why not send them a message. Maybe something like:

Hi, (Personalize it by putting the person's name here)! My name is Matthew Davenport, and I'm the author of the novel The Trials of Obed Marsh. *I saw that you added it to your To-Read shelf and I wanted thank you for your interest in my book.*

If you happen to have the time, I have a few e-book copies of the book that are available to give away, and I would like to exchange them for genuine reviews on Goodreads and Amazon.com (provide the links). If you're interested, I can email you the book.

Either way, I am genuinely grateful in your interest in my book.

Thank you,

Matt

I have had some great conversations from messages like this.

Also, don't forget to check out the groups on Goodreads, some of my best discussions and sales pitches have happened on those message boards.

Author Marketing Club (AuthorMarketingClub.com):

Author Marketing Club is a great resource for educating yourself on how to do a lot of the processes involved in self-publishing. It also has a forum where you can ask for reviews.

This is a book about doing things for free, and I only have a free membership on Author Marketing Club as of the writing of this book, but you should be aware that while there are so many great resources on the free side of Author Marketing Club, the paid subscription has even more resources, including the Reviewer Grabber Tool. The Reviewer Grabber Tool searches through the Amazon's Top Reviewers and helps you locate people who will review your books. I hear that it's awesome, but also hit and miss.

Returning to the free option, there are a ton of great lessons on the site that can help you through so many problems that you might face during your process. The community is another great resource. There are so many people, just like you, trying to make it big in this crazy world.

IFTTT:

This one is my favorite because it does the work for you.

IFTTT (If This Then That) is a website that allows you to create simple formulas to automate the internet. That sounds complicated but it isn't.

For example, if I wanted to have a specific tweet go out once a day, I would go to IFTTT.com and create a recipe. First I would start with this "This" trigger, which would be the clock (indicating a specific time). I would set the time and day or days. Then I would set up the "That" action, which would be Twitter. Once I'm finished, it would post a tweet every day at the same time.

You can use this with so many different tools, including Facebook and any blog that you might have.

Makeuseof.com has a great tutorial on IFTTT at http://www.makeuseof.com/tag/the-ultimate-ifttt-guide-use-the-webs-most-powerful-tool-like-a-pro/ .

We have very busy schedules and the more we can have the internet doing the work for us, the more time that we can spend on getting back to writing.

Part 8: Free Is A Lie

Lies...: The Imagined Contract

A lot of people like to use free as a marketing tactic and, done correctly, it can be. Unfortunately, it isn't always done correctly.

Some services, specifically Amazon's KDP Select, give you the option to have promotional free days for your books. The idea is that possibly thousands of readers will grab up your free books, read them, and then give you reviews or buy your other books. In a perfect world, this would be the case.

That's the Imagined Contract. The only part of the Imagined Contract that actually happens is that people will grab up your book with a ferocity. Unfortunately, your free audience isn't going to be the same as your normal audience. Your free audience is actually made up of people who saw that a free book was available and might be interested in reading it later, so they grab it while it's free and it will most likely end up sitting on their reader for a while before they look at it again.

So, you've given away however-many copies of your books and you haven't received many (if any) more reviews. Not to mention, if you're tracking your actual sales, you'll notice that you didn't average out any higher than usual.

That's because the free audience didn't sign the Imagined Contract and don't have to follow through with your hopes and dreams. They just wanted a free e-book.

To be fair, some people will go ahead and give you reviews and possibly buy your other books. Unfortunately, I sincerely doubt it.

The reason that it doesn't work (in my humble opinion) is because it's a marketing plan that doesn't involve the most important thing about marketing: Engagement.

Sales happen when you engage your audience, and buy giving out your book for free to thousands of people you're not engaging anyone. Instead, you're just giving away your book.

Instead, focus on marketing plans that encourage engagement.

I just discovered Wattpad.com right before I started writing this book. Wattpad is a site that allows you to subscribe to people's stories for free. In this case, free works to drive sales because each story has a comments section and readers are encouraged to interact with the authors of the stories they read. Don't believe me? Google Search for "Wattpad success story." When you can engage your readers, free works. They feel like they're part of the process, they form a relationship with you and now they want to read your other works.

Engagement is key.

...And More Lies: The Ranking Lie

You might be thinking that at least, if you give away a ton of books, you will get to move up the author ranks. Thousands of downloads means you're better than everyone else, right?

Unfortunately, wrong.

Your overall author ranking won't change unless people pay for your books. Your free books only move you up in the free rankings, and it's a lot harder to make it to the top of that list.

Don't do it for the ranking, because unless you can convert those free downloads into paid purchases, it really doesn't mean much.

On the flip side, the more downloads that you get on Wattpad.com, the higher you move in ranking on that page, and a higher rank means higher visibility. With more visibility you can engage more and more readers.

Engagement is key. I can't emphasize this enough.

The Pricing Sweet Spot

What if I told you that you could make more sales without making your book free?

Well, it's true.

Smashwords.com put out a graph showing their book sales and the price points that each book sold at.

While free and $0.99 books still get downloaded in high volumes, the largest volume of downloads is for books in the $2.99 to the $4.99 range.

I can even vouch for this on a personal level. My novels all sell better when I put them at a price point in the "Smashwords Range," than when I give them away. My book *The Statement of Andrew Doran* was only $0.99 for over a month and I sold more books before and after that month than I did during it.

This is because of 'Perceived Value.'

Perceived Value is the value that a consumer assumes that the product has. Many things can change the Perceived Value, including cover design, how well marketed your book is, the book description, and the cost.

When I say cost, I specifically mean that if a book is costs nothing people will assume that it probably isn't worth anything. That's unfortunate, because you didn't put all of that work into it for nothing and you need to be compensated for the work that you produce.

Unfortunately, it doesn't work 100% in the other direction. Just because you think the work that you put into your book is worth a million bucks, doesn't mean that you can charge that much. You should take a look at what other books in your genre are selling for and make a judgment based on that. If the bestsellers in your genre are going for $3.99, then you should probably aim for around that price point instead of trying to retrain your potential audience.

Earlier, I said that free was a bad idea unless done right. The best way to do it right is with a series. If you have a series, you can usually get away with giving away only the first book in the series. That will get people to read your first book and if they like it they will hopefully buy the next in your series. People buy what they like, and in this instance free is a great marketing tool, because you're specifically using it to sell the rest of the books in your series.

Part 9: Don't Stop There

Audio Books, Comic Books, Short Stories, And More...

Your book is all the stores, your price is decent, your cover didn't make children cry, and you're about to start writing your next book, so I guess that you can say goodbye to this book.

Right?

Oh, heck no!

There's so much more you can do. Your babies might be off to college, but wouldn't you like to make their lives the best that you can?

Here are some other things that you can do with your books.

- Make an audio book. Go on over to Amazon's ACX.com and load your book up. Audio books done through ACX have multiple ways to pay the producer, and one of them is a Royalty Share. Royalty Share means that you don't have to pay the producer up front as long as you're alright with sharing the royalties from the audio book with the producer. It's also a fun process. There is nothing quite as exciting as hearing someone else read your work out loud.

- Make a comic book. I haven't done this one, but I'm currently thinking about it. There are a lot of sites to find artists, including DeviantArt and Reddit. However you do it, this one won't be free, unless you can find a royalty share option similar to ACX. If you do, please email me and I'll add it to the revised editions of this book. In short, you're going to have to start pitching people, either from DeviantArt, Reddit, or Wherever, the idea for your novel. Don't sweat it and be proud of your work.

● Write Short Stories. Probably one of the best marketing tools out there is to write more stories. Specifically, you've just created a vast world that might even span multiple books, so why not write supplemental stories for that work and pass those out for free? Earlier, I mentioned that the best use of free is as a marketing tool, and this is another way to use it. Write a short story prequel or maybe a short back story to one of the more subtle characters (Star Wars did this with every one of those bounty hunters you saw in The Empire Strikes Back), and put it up on Wattpad or wherever for free. This is fun both for you and the audience. You'll get to play in the sandbox again, and your audience will get to see your story through fresh new material.

And More (read that with a Dramatic Voice)! There's so much more that you can do with your story. Podcast interviews, TV interviews, book signings, readings at local libraries, wine tours, pub crawls, Reddit AMA's (Ask Me Anything), and writing groups. The point is to engage, but how you do it is up to you. As long as you're sharing your love of the world or worlds that you've created with your audience, it doesn't matter how you engage. The excitement is contagious and your fans will love it.

Marketing Is A Full-Time Job

One final note is that Marketing is a Full-time job, but you don't have to treat it like that.

Almost everyone who reads this is going to go check Facebook or Twitter or whatever site they prefer at least a billion more times before the year ends. Posting a link to your book or to an interview you did only takes a second of your time. After a while (mileage may vary) you won't have to market your books, you'll be marketing yourself, and your fans will just buy your books as you announce them.

That's the dream anyway.

In the end, as long as you engage and work your booty off you will see results.

Part 10: Outroduction...?

So Long And Good Luck

That's everything that I have for you.

Well, that's not true, I could go on and on for days about the virtues of self-publishing, who to approach about book signings, and the strength of a local community of authors, but that's not the point of this book.

The point of this book was to show you the paths that you could take if you wanted to avoid spending money during your process.

Have I ever spent money on my novels?

Yes.

Only once. I ran a Pubslush Campaign (http://andrewdoran.pubslush.com) to raise money so that my editor (who I had never paid previously) could finally afford groceries. So, have I ever spent money on my novels? Yes. Was it my money? Nope, it was contributor money. Pubslush is a crowd-funding platform just like Kickstarter (kickstarter.com) that focuses on helping independent publishers raise money for their works.

Most importantly, I hope that you were able to take something away from this book.

Such as:

- Inexpensive doesn't mean "Cheap."
- You don't need to spend money to produce a professional product.
- If you don't spend money, you will spend time, sweat, and stress.
- But it will be worth it.

Once again, this was meant to be a map guiding you down the road of least cost. I hope that you have found at least one resource in here that has made this entire work worth it for you.

About the Author

Matthew Davenport lives in Des Moines, Iowa with his beautiful wife, Ren. He spends his time writing, reading, and working to promote and support writing communities in Iowa through his company Davenport Writes, LLC.

You can keep track of Matthew through his twitter account @spazenport.

You can follow his blog at http://davenportwrites.com